Insults and put downs

For my 3 lovely ladies.

Politicians

Something about a political insult is exceptionally gratifying. Whether it be that we like to sense humour in our policy makers, or we see their wit as refreshing, political insults and comebacks are often remembered. We enjoy a good response and a quick exchange and of course we like to see the politicians who rile us, take a verbal pasting from their opposition. Some are subtle, some less so, but for centuries politicians across the world have been delivering some of the finest put downs in history.

Benjamin Disraeli on Gladstone: *"He has not one single redeeming defect."*

Benjamin Disraeli on Gladstone: *"Inebriated with the exuberance of his own verbosity, and gifted with an egotistical imagination."*

Benjamin Disraeli on Robert Peel: *"The right honourable gentlemen's smile is like the silver fittings of a coffin."*

Benjamin Disraeli on Robert Peel: *"The right honourable gentleman is reminiscent of a poker. The only difference is that a poker gives off the occasional signs of warmth."*

Benjamin Disraeli on John Russel: *"If a traveller were informed that such a man were leader of the House of Commons, he may well begin to comprehend how the Egyptians worshipped an insect."*

Benjamin Disraeli on the difference between a misfortune and a calamity: *"The difference between a misfortune and a calamity is this: If Gladstone fell into the Thames, it would be a misfortune. But if someone dragged him out again, that would be a calamity."*

John Bright on Benjamin Disraeli: *"He is a self-made man and worships his creator."*

John Montagu: *"Sir, I do not know whether you will die on the gallows or of the pox!"*
John Wilkes: *"That, sir, depends on whether I first embrace your Lordship's principles or your Lordship's mistresses."*

David Lloyd George on Sir John Simon: *"The right honourable and learned gentleman has twice crossed the floor of this House, each time leaving behind a trail of slime."*

David Lloyd George on the House of Lords: *"A body of 500 men chosen at random from amongst the unemployed."*

Lord Beaverbrook's Butler: *"The Lord is out walking"*
Lloyd George: *"Ah, on the water, I presume"*

Winston Churchill: *"The best argument against democracy is a five-minute conversation with the average voter."*

Winston Churchill on Stanley Baldwin: *"He occasionally stumbled over the truth, but hastily picked himself up and hurried on as if nothing had happened."*

Lady Astor: *"Winston, if I were your wife I'd put poison in your coffee."*
Winston Churchill: *"Nancy, if I were your husband I'd drink it."*

Winston Churchill on being disturbed on the toilet by the Lord Privy Seal: *"Tell him I can only deal with one shit at a time"*

A since disputed, however deliciously contemptuous comment came in an exchange between Churchill and Sir Bernard Shaw – we really hope he said it.

Shaw *"Here are two tickets for the opening of my new play. Keep one for yourself and bring along a friend—if you can find one."*

Churchill *"I'm sorry that a previous engagement precludes my attending your opening night. I shall be happy to come the second night—if there is one."*

Labour MP Bessie Braddock to Churchill: *"Winston, you're drunk!"*
Churchill: *"Bessie, you're ugly, and tomorrow morning I shall be sober"*

Winston Churchill on the Labour Party: *"They are not fit to manage a whelk stall."*

Winston Churchill on Stanley Baldwin: *"I wish Stanley Baldwin no ill, but it would have been much better if he had never lived."*

Winston Churchill on Clement Attlee: *"A modest man, who has much to be modest about."*

Winston Churchill on Neville Chamberlain: *""An appeaser is one who feeds a crocodile hoping it will eat him last."*

Winston Churchill on Prime Minister Lord Rosebery: *"He was a great man in an era of small events."*

Winston Churchill on Clement Attlee: *"An empty cab pulled up to Downing Street. Clement Attlee got out."*

Aneurin Sevan on Clement Attlee: *"He brings to the fierce struggle of politics the tepid enthusiasm of a lazy summer afternoon at a cricket match."*

Balfour on Churchill: *"I thought he was a young man of promise; but it appears he was a young man of promises."*

Charles de Gaul on Winston Churchill: *"When I am right, I get angry. Churchill gets angry when he is wrong. We are angry at each other much of the time"*

Tony Banks on Terry Dicks: *"The honorable Member is living proof that a pig's bladder on a stick can be elected to Parliament."*

Tony Banks on Terry Dicks: *"Listening to Terry Dicks opining on the arts is rather like listening to Vlad the Impaler presenting Blue Peter."*

Dennis Healey on Geoffrey Howe: *"Like being savaged by a dead sheep."*

Dennis Healey: *"Mrs. Thatcher tells us she has given the French President a piece of her mind….. not a gift I would receive with alacrity."*

James Callaghan *"May I congratulate you on being the only man in your team."*
Margaret Thatcher *"That's one more than you've got in yours."*

Margaret Thatcher on Neil Kinnock: *"You don't reach Downing Street by pretending you've travelled the road to Damascus when you haven't even left home."*

Ken Clarke: *"Isn't it terrible about losing to the Germans at our national sport?"*
Margaret Thatcher: *"I shouldn't worry too much – we've beaten them twice this Century at theirs."*

Tony Banks: *"[She behaves] with the sensitivity of a sex-starved boa constrictor."*

William Whitelaw on Harold Wilson: *"He is going around the country stirring up apathy."*

Norman Tebbit on Dennis Skinner: *"Far better to keep your mouth shut and let everyone think you're stupid than to open it and leave no doubt."*

Jonathan Aitken Margaret Thatcher: *"She probably thinks Sinai is the plural of sinus."*

Gerald Kaufman on Edwina Currie; *"Mrs. Currie loses an enormous amount of opportunities to stay silent."*

Nicholas Fairburn to Edwina Currie during the salmonella crisis: *"Does the Honourable Lady remember that she was an egg herself once: and very many members of all sides of this House regret that it was ever fertilised?"*

Frank Dobson: *"When Edwina Currie goes to the dentist, he needs the anaesthetic."*

Stephen Glover on John Major: *"He delivers all his statements as though auditioning for the speaking clock."*

John Prescott on John Major: *"John Major is to leadership what Cyril Smith is to Han gliding."*

Tony Banks on William Hague: *"And now, to make matters worse, they (the Tories) have elected a foetus as party leader. I bet a lot of them wish they had not voted against abortion now! "*

Tony Banks on John Major: *"...so unpopular, if he became a funeral director people would stop dying."*

Tony Banks on Michael Portillo: *"At one point Portillo was polishing his jackboots and planning the next advance. And the next thing is he shows up as a TV presenter. It is rather like Pol Pot presenting the Teletubbies."*

Arthur Scargill on Ken Livingstone: *" I wouldn't vote for Ken Livingstone if he were running for mayor of toy town."*

John Junor on Margaret Beckett: *"Not even her best friends would describe her as a glamour puss whose face would be likely to turn on many voters. Except perhaps those who are members of the British Horse Society."*

Nigel Farage on European President Herman Van Rompuy: *"I don't want to be rude but, really, you have the charisma of a damp rag and the appearance of a low-grade bank clerk."*

Vince Cable to Gordon Brown: *"The house has noticed the prime minister's remarkable transformation in the last few weeks from Stalin to Mr Bean"*

President Obama referencing Sarah Palin's comment on 'soccer mums and lipstick': *"You can put lipstick on a pig...it's still a pig."*

Bob Dole: *"History buffs probably noted the reunion at a Washington party a few weeks ago of three ex-presidents: Carter, Ford, and Nixon -- See No Evil, Hear No Evil, and Evil."*

Lyndon Johnson on Gerald Ford: *"He's a nice guy, but he played too much football with his helmet off."*

Reporter to Gandhi: *"What do you think of Western Civilisation?"*
Gandhi: *"I think it would be a good idea."*

Abraham Lincoln on Stephen Douglas: *"His argument is as thin as the homeopathic soup that was made by boiling the shadow of a pigeon that had been starved to death."*

Golda Meir on Moshe Dayan: *"Don't be so humble, you're not that great."*

Tom Clancy: *"Bill Clinton is a man who thinks international affairs means dating a girl from out of town."*

Barney Frank on Gerorge W Bush: *"People might cite George Bush as proof that you can be totally impervious to the effects of a Harvard and Yale education."*

Pat Buchanan on Bill Clinton: *"Bill Clinton's foreign policy experience is pretty much confined to having had breakfast once at the International House of Pancakes."*

Ann Richards on George W. Bush: *"Poor George, he can't help it. He was born with a silver foot in his mouth."*

Jim Hightower, former Texas Commissioner of Agriculture: *"If ignorance goes to forty dollars a barrel, I want drilling rights to George Bush's head."*

Stephen Colbert on George W Bush: *"I stand by this man because he stands for things. Not only for things, he stands on things. Things like aircraft carriers, and rubble, and recently flooded city squares. And that sends a strong message that no matter what happens to America she will always rebound with the most powerfully staged photo-ops in the world."*

Jack Kemp on Bob Dole: *"In a recent fire Bob Dole's library burned down. Both books were lost. And he hadn't even finished coloring one of them."*

Teddy Roosevelt on President William McKinley: *"No more backbone than a chocolate éclair."*

Paul Keating on John Hewson: *"He's like a shiver waiting for a spine."*

Paul Keating on John Howard *"What we have got is a dead carcass, swinging in the breeze, but nobody will cut it down to replace him."*

Paul Keating on John Howard *"I am not like the Leader of the Opposition. I did not slither out of the Cabinet room like a mangy maggot..."*

Paul Keating on John Howard: *"...the brain-damaged Leader of the Opposition..."*

Paul Keating on Wilson Tuckey: *"You boxhead you wouldn't know. You are flat out counting past ten."*

Paul Keating on debating John Hewson: *"like being flogged with a warm lettuce."*

Paul Keating on John Hewson: *"I was implying that the Honorable Member for Wentworth was like a lizard on a rock - alive, but looking dead."*

Paul Keating on Andrew Peacock: *"I suppose that the Honourable Gentleman's hair, like his intellect, will recede into the darkness."*

Paul Keating on Andrew Peacock: *"...what we have here is an intellectual rust bucket."*

Paul Keating on Andrew Peacock: *"...if this gutless spiv, and I refer to him as a gutless spiv..."*

Paul Keating on Ian Sinclair: *"What we have as a leader of the National Party is a political carcass with a coat and tie on."*

Harold L. Ickes on Huey Long: *"The trouble with Senator Long is that he is suffering from halitosis of the intellect."*

Mark Twain: *"Reader, suppose you were an idiot. Now suppose you were a member of Congress. But I repeat myself."*

@ConanOBrien: *I picked out my Halloween costume. I'm going as 'Slutty Madeleine Albright'*
@madeleineAlbright: *@conanObrien I'm considering going as hunky Conan O'Brien – but that might be too far fetched....*

David Cameron on Tony Blair: *"He was the future once."*

Barack Obama on the uber tanned speaker of the house: *"These days, the House Republicans actually give John Boehner a harder time than they give me. Which means orange really is the new black.*

Interviewer on John McCains war hero status: *"He is a war hero because he was captured."*
Donald Trump: *"I like people that weren't captured."*

While we like our Politicians to be quick witted, we probably prefer a bumbling politician who gets what he deserves. Comments like the one above from 'The Donald', Donald trump, have made him something of a hapless victim of other peoples' wit.

Bette Middler via twitter: *"60 Shades of Stupidity: Ten extra points for the terrible dye job someone talked him into."*

Seth Meyers: "Donald Trump has been saying he will run for president as a Republican, which is surprising because I just assumed that he was running as a joke,"

President Obama, following Trump's demands to see his birth certificate to check that the president was born in the USA: "I know that he's taken some flak lately, but nobody is prouder to put this birth certificate matter to rest than The Donald and that's because he can finally get back to focusing on the issues that matter, like: did we fake the moon landing? What really happened in Roswell? And where are Biggie and Tupac?"

Seth Meyers: "Donald Trump often appears on Fox, which is ironic because a fox often appears on Donald Trump's head."

Cher: "Donald Trump Can't come up with a hairstyle that looks human, how can he come up with a plan to defeat ISIS."

Jimmy Kimmel: "The closest Trump ever got to battle was his fight with Rosie O'Donnell."

Donald Trump: "Places in London are so radicalised police refuse to go there."
Boris Johnson: "Crime has been falling steadily in both London and New York- the only reason I wouldn't go to some parts of New York is the real risk of meeting Donald Trump."

Trump often reacts badly to his detractors, one notable exchange occurred between him and Modern Family writer Danny Zuker on twitter, with Zuker emerging the clearly superior wit.

Trump: "I've been warning about China since as early as the 80's. No one wanted to listen. Now our country is in real trouble. #Timetogettough."
Zuker: "You've always been tough on China Sir. Particularly the children who make your shitty clothes."

Trump: *"Danny – you're a total loser."*

Zuker: *"Your insults need work. Here's one I have been working on. "Every picture you post of yourself is a dick pic." See?*

Trump: *"I can't resist hitting lightweight @Dannyzuker verbally when he starts up because he is just so pathetic and easy (stupid)*

Zuker: *"Since you are unable to manufacture decent comebacks maybe you should outsource the job to China #LOL #Trumplestiltskin*

Trump: *"Lightweight @Dannyzuker is too stupid to see that China (and others) is destroying the US economically and our leaders are helpless. SAD*

Zuker: *"I'm def too stupid to see how manufacturing your shitty clothes in China while you bloviate about them isn't hypocritical."*

Trump: *"Just tried watching modern family- written by a moron, really boring. Writer has the mind of a very dumb and backward child. Sorry Danny."*

Zuker: *"@realdonaldtrump doesn't like the show I work on but then we never tested well with the racist, hypocritical, multi bankruptcy demo."*

Trump: *" WHO ON EARTH IS DANNY ZUKER???!!!! A lightweight moron who only gets attention by attacking Trump."*

Zuker: *" Clearly the one thing @realdonaldtrump didn't inherit from his daddy was a thesaurus. #Loser #dummy #lightweight."*

Royalty

Royalty have always been a target for insulting comments, however it is certainly not unknown for them to give as god as they get.

Rudyard Kipling on Edward VII: *"A corpulent voluptuary."*

John Wesley on Elizabeth I: *"As just and merciful as Nero and as good a Christian as Mohammed."*

James Keir Hardie on George V *"Born into the ranks of the working class, the new King's most likely fate would have been that of a street-corner loafer."*

Harold Nicolson on George V: *"For seventeen years he did nothing at all but kill animals and stick in stamps."*

Prince Albert on Edward, Prince of Wales: *"His intellect is of no more use than a pistol packed in the bottom of a trunk in the robber infested Apennines."*

Henry VIII when first meeting Anne of Cleves: *"You have sent me a Flanders mare."*

Bette Midler on Princess Anne: *"She loves nature, in spite of what it did to her."*

Neil Kinnock: *"I am prepared to take advice on leisure from Prince Philip. He is a world expert on leisure. He's been practising for most of his adult life."*

King George V *" I thought men like that shot themselves."*

Alfred De Marigny on Edward VIII: *"A pimple on the arse of the Empire."*

Prince Philip on Ethiopian Art: *"It looks like the kind of thing my daughter would bring back from her school art lessons."*

Prince Philip to a Scottish driving instructor: *"How do you keep the natives off the booze long enough to pass the test?"*

Prince Philip to deaf children stood near a steel band: *"If you're near that music it's no wonder you're deaf".*

Prince Philip to a fashion designer: *"You didn't design your beard too well, did you? You really must try better with your beard."*

Prince Philip on Princess Anne: *"If it doesn't fart or eat hay then she isn't interested"*

The Arts

Whether It be the theatre or literature or the world of Hollywood, those that pour their souls into the arts are perhaps the most prone to very quotable turns of phrase. Jealousies and egos have often combined to produce so fabulous comebacks and insults.

Dorothy Parker on Audrey Hepburn: *"She ran the whole gamut of the emotions from A to B."*

Alan Bennett on Arianna Stassinopoulos: *"So boring, you fall asleep halfway through her name"*

Frank Sinatra on Robert Redford: *"Well, at least he has found his true love – what a pity he can't marry himself."*

Liberace to a critic*: "Thank you for your very amusing review. After reading it I cried all the way to the bank."*

Bill Murray to Chevy Chase: *"Medium talent!"*

Katherine Hepburn on Sharon Stone: *"It's a new low for actresses when you have to wonder what's between her ears instead of her legs."*

Elizabeth Taylor *"Richard Burton is so discriminating that he won't go to see a play with anybody in it but himself."*

Sir John Gielgud on Ingrid Bergman: *"She speaks five languages and can't act in any of them."*

Kathy Griffin on Angelina Jolie: *"Her lips look like an inflamed anus."*

Dorothy Parker: *"That woman speaks eighteen languages and can't say 'no' in any of them."*

Elizabeth Taylor: *"Some of my best leading men have been dogs and horses."*

Joan Rivers: *"Elizabeth Taylor was so fat that whenever she went to London in a red dress, 30 passengers would try to board her."*

Joan Rivers: *"Elizabeth Taylor is so fat she puts mayonnaise on her asprin"*

Bette Davis on Joan Crawford: *"You should never say bad things about the dead, you should only say good... Joan Crawford is dead. Good."*

Bette Davis on Joan Crawford *"She has slept with every male star at MGM except Lassie."*

Bette Davis on Joan Crawford: *"Joan Crawford — Hollywood's first case of syphilis."*

Bette Davis: *"Why am I so good at playing bitches? I think it's because I'm not a bitch. Maybe that's why Joan Crawford always plays ladies."*

Bette Davis *"I have always admired Katherine Hepburn's cheekbones – more than her films."*

Bette Davis on Miriam Hopkins: *"God was very good to the world, he took her from us."*

Joan Crawford on Bette Davis: *"Miss Davis was always partial to covering up her face in motion pictures. She called it 'art.' Others might call it camouflage"*

Tallulah Bankhead on Bette Davis: *"Don't think I don't know who's been spreading gossip about me. After all the nice things I've said about that hag. When I get hold of her, I'll tear out every hair of her mustache!"*

Rex Harrison on Charlton Heston: *"Charlton Heston is good at playing arrogance and ambition. But in the same way that a dwarf is good at being short."*

Mary Anderson to Alfred Hitchcock: *""What is my best side Mr Hitchcock?"*
Hitchcock: *"You're sitting on it, my dear."*

Richard Harris on Michael Caine: *"An over-fat, flatulent, 62-year-old windbag. A master of inconsequence masquerading as a guru, passing off his vast limitations as pious virtues."*

Sharon Stone on Gwyneth Paltrow: *"She's very young and lives in rarefied air that's a little thin. It's like she's not getting quite enough oxygen."*

W.C. Fields on Mae West: *"A plumber's idea of Cleopatra."*

Dorothy Parker: *"Marion Davies has two expressions — joy and indigestion."*

Clare Luce, holding a door for Dorothy Parker: *"Age before beauty."*
Dorothy Parker, walking through: *"Pearls before swine."*

George S. Kaufman: *"I saw the play at a disadvantage — the curtain was up."*

Christopher Plummer on Julie Andrews: *"Working with her is like being hit over the head with a big Valentine's Day card, every day."*

Burt Lancaster: *"Kirk Douglas would be the first to tell you he is a difficult man, I would be the second."*

Tallulah Bankhead to Tennessee Williams: *"Darling, they've absolutely ruined your perfectly dreadful play."*

Tallulah Bankhead on Bette Davis: *"There's nothing I wouldn't say to her face, both of them."*

George Burns: *"Carol Channing never just enters a room. Even when she comes out of the bathroom, her husband applauds."*

Dorothy Parker on Harold Ross: *"His ignorance was an Empire State Building of ignorance. You had to admire it for its size."*

Noel Coward: *"Edna, you look almost like a man."*
Edna Ferber: *"So do you."*

George S. Kaufman: *"Saw your performance tonight from the back of the house. Wish you were here."*

Alexander Woollcott when asked to sign his book: "Ah, what is so rare as a Woollcott first edition!"
Franklin Pierce Adams: "A Woollcott second edition."

Groucho Marx could account for a book by himself; some of his best insults are quoted below

"He may look like an idiot and talk like an idiot, but don't let that fool you. He really is an idiot."

"I have nothing but respect for you …and not much of that."

"I never forget a face, but in your case I'd be glad to make an exception."

"From the moment I picked your book up until I laid it down, I was convulsed with laughter. Someday I intend to read it."

"I've had a perfectly wonderful evening, but this wasn't it."

"Marry me and I'll never look at another horse!"

Tennessee Williams: "Truman Capote had a voice so high it could only be detected by a bat."

Mark Twain on Lilian Aldrich: *"I do not believe I could learn to like her except on a raft at sea with no other provisions in sight"*

Kathy Griffin on Renee Zellweger: *"I don't think she has eaten since Chicago. She is like the lost Olsen triplet."*

Mark Twain: *"I didn't attend the funeral, but I sent a nice letter saying I approve of it."*

Oscar Levant: *""Every time I look at you I get a fierce desire to be lonesome."*

George Bernard Shaw: "The trouble with her is that she lacks the power of conversation but not the power of speech."

Leonora Corbett: "There goes the original good time that's been had by all."

Voltaire: *"Your manuscript was both good and original. Unfortunately the bit that was good was not original, and the bit that was original was not good."*

Sharon Osbourne on Nicole Kidman: *"Her forehead looks like a flatscreen TV."*

Lindsay Lohan on Keria Knightley: *"That flat chested cardboard cut-out."*

Joan Collins on Linda Evans: *"It's quite off putting having to look at that face."*

Marlon Brando on James Dean: *"Mr. Dean appears to be wearing my last year's wardrobe and using my last year's talent."*

Richard Burton on Marlon Brando: *"Marlon has yet to learn to speak. He should have been born two generations before and acted in silent films."*

Sophia Loren on Gina Lollobrigida: *"Gina's personality is limited. She is good playing a peasant but is incapable of playing a lady."*

Richard Harris on Michael Caine: *"An over-fat, flatulent, 62-year-old windbag. A master of inconsequence masquerading as a guru, passing off his vast limitations as pious virtues."*

Julia Roberts: *"Gwyneth Paltrow is quite pretty in a British horsey sort of way."*

Peter Bogdanovich: *"Working with Cher was like being in a blender with an alligator."*

Ben Stiller on Owen Wilson: *"That's when I realised we were a comedy duo, when I saw Behind Enemy Lines I realised Owen Wilson should never be alone."*

Fan: *@FrankieMuniz Ur acting is just, awful, sorry but it is.*
Frankie Muniz: *Yeah, but being retired with $40,000,000.00 at 19 has not been awful. Good luck moving out of your moms house before you're 35.*

Edward Porter: *"Johnny Depp puts the dire in director."*

Michael Medved: *"Farrah Fawcett is uniquely suited to play a woman of limited intelligence."*

Ernest Hemingway: *"Any picture in which Errol Flynn is the best actor is its own worst enemy."*

Leslie Halliwell on Blake Edwards: *"A man of many talents, all of them minor."*

W. C Fields on Mae West: *"A plumber's idea of Cleopatra."*

Jack De Manio on Glenda Jackson: *"She has a face to launch a thousand dredgers."*

Noel Coward to Claudette Colbert: *"I would wring your neck…. If you had one."*

Harry Andrews: *"Who could forget Mel Gibson in Hamlet? Though many have tried.*

Kenneh Tynan on Roman Polanski: *"The four-foot Pole you wouldn't want to touch with a ten-foot pole."*

Dorothy Parker: *"If you don't knit, bring a good book."*

Dorothy Parker: *"This is not a novel to be tossed aside lightly. It should be thrown with great force."*

Dorothy Parker: *"This must be a gift book: That is to say, a book which you wouldn't take under any other terms."*

Dorothy Parker: *"This book of essays…. Has all the depth and glitter of a worn dime."*

Dorothy Parker: *"I know who wrote the lyrics and I know the names of the people in the cast, but I'm not going to tell on them."*

Ilka Chase: *"Not only was Clare (Booth)loyal to her friends she was very kind to her inferiors*
Dorothy Parker: *"And where does she find them?"*

The Soaps

Soap writers quickly established that acerbic retorts and acidic put downs were part of a formula that ensured a soap baddy was a popular one. J.R Ewing, played to perfection by Larry Hagman in Dallas, became the yardstick against which all other writers measured their creations. Some of his more memorable comments are reflected below. Fans of insults should consider purchasing Dallas on DVD

"Ray never was comfortable eating with the family; we do use knives and forks."

J.R on Ray

"Say, why don't you have that junior plastic surgeon you married design you a new face: one without a mouth!"

J.R to his cousin Lucy

"Mary Lee, if you don't hurry, someone else is gonna get your street corner!"

J.R at his politically correct best

"You should go to sleep Sue Ellen, you know how haggard you look when you don't get your full eight hours!?"

J.R to long suffering wife Sue Ellen.

Cliff: *"We are related!"*
J.R: *"We're not even the same specie Barnes!"*
J.R to long term enemy and brother in law Cliff Barnes.

Dynasty's Alexis, played by Joan Collins, took the art of the insult to whole new levels thanks to excellent script writing and perfect delivery which combined to make Alexis, like J.R a soap icon. Again, Dynasty is available on DVD and the insults alone make it a great watch.

Alexis to her daughter Fallon: *"I'm glad to see that your father had your teeth fixed... if not your tongue."*

Alexis: *"Like your wardrobe, Mr Hess, your sense of humour is not your strong suit."*

Alexis: "I'm negotiating to buy the Carlton Hotel."
Dominique: "I've heard – that's why I was in such a hurry to move out."
Alexis: "Yes well it was never meant to be a hotel for transients."

Alexis's best invective however was usually reserved for her ex-husband's new wife, Krystle.

Alexis : " *I loved that outfit when I first saw it. I'm amazed it lasted so many seasons."*

Krystle: *"I'm not here to gloat."*
Alexis: *"Perhaps you'd like to look at our new collection. We have some lovely things……. Some of them might even fit you."*

Krystle: *"Any notes I take (at the meeting) will be for a press release – I'll be sure to send you a copy."*
Alexis: *"Well that's very considerate of you – I can't wait to read your first attempt at literacy."*

Alexis: *"Are you pregnant?"*
Krystle: *"Yes."*
Alexis: *"Congratulations … though it's not that special – even worms can procreate."*

Alexis: *"Krystle – imagine seeing you in front of the jewellers. Are you here to buy or sell?"*

However, by the later seasons Alexis was given a more equal character to trade abuse with in the form of Sable Colby, played by Stephanie Beacham, their exchanges became legendary.

Alexis: *"Oh, my God, don't tell me you're still here. I thought you were just a temporary infestation."*
Sable: *"Well, Alexis, I see you survived Africa. It's a dangerous place for most animals, but no problem for you of course."*
Alexis: *"The sable's an animal too, you know, from the rodent family."*
Sable: *"Mm, speaking of the rodent family... how are you Adam? Come to visit mummy? Hope you're not trying to climb out onto the weakest limb of the family tree – especially when it's about to fall on the ground."*

Alexis: *"No I won't have any coffee, thank you."*
Sable: *"Not even laced with something?"*

Sable (as Adam and Alexis stand at her door): *"You two? Good Lord, Alexis, I don't know why you don't grow and pouch and carry him around like a kangaroo."*
Alexis: *"A pouch? You mean like the one you're developing?"*

Alexis: *"Why did you buy my hotel? "*
Sable Colby: *"But that's what Pavilian Resorts does, darling. It acquires run-down properties that have been poorly maintained, like yourself."*

Sable: *"Who would have thought Roger Grimes would come floating up after 20 years."*
Alexis: *"He was always unpredictable....A bullet has the strangest habit of making even the liveliest people seem dead. Now would you please take your hand off the (elevator) button because I don't have time for the dead or the dull."*

Alexis: *"Women don't kill men who are madly in love with them Sable, and if anyone had been madly in love with you, you would understand that."*

Sable: *"You don't know when to stop, do you?"*
Alexis: *"Oh yes I do – when I hear the thump, thump, thump of driving over something hard and empty ... like your head."*

Sable: *"Jet lag has apparently dimmed your bulb more than usual, Alexis."*

Alexis: *"I just love the way you stand by your men, Sable. What a pity they won't lie down with you."*

Sable: *"You're drunk."*
Alexis: *"That may be, but tomorrow I'll be sober while you, alas, will still be you."*

Alexis: *"Did you really think I wouldn't find out about that Stahl picture? The one that drained the colour from your already pallid face?"*

Comedy programmes

Perhaps inspired by the soaps, in the 80s and 90s, comedy writers developed the insult and put down into something more, and few people did it better than the team behind Blackadder. By allowing Blackadder, played by Rowan Atkinson a variety of annoying sidekicks, they created opportunity after opportunity for hilarious putdowns.

Blackadder

'Your brain for example- is so minute, Baldrick, that if a hungry cannibal cracked your head open, there wouldn't be enough to cover a small water biscuit.'

'To you, Baldrick, the Rennaissance was just something that happened to other people, wasn't it?'

'The eyes are open, the mouth moves, but Mr Brain has long since departed, hasn't he, Percy?'

"They do say, Mrs M, that verbal insults hurt more than physical pain. They are, of course, wrong, as you will soon discover when I stick this toasting fork into your head."

'I lost closer friends than "darling Georgie" the last time I was deloused.'

'Baldrick, your head is as empty as a eunuch's underpants.'

'It's so dirty, it would be unacceptable to a dung beetle who had lost interest in its career and really let itself go.'

"You find yourself amusing, Blackadder."
"I try not to fly in the face of public opinion."

"I don't take kindly to insults."
"Funny, with a face like yours, I'd have thought you'd be used to it by now."

In a similar vein, long suffering Basil Fawlty's insults kept us laughing as he dealt with a string of obnoxious guests and his tyrannical wife.

Sybil: *"Don't shout at me. I've had a difficult morning."*
Basil: *"Oh, dear, what happened? Did you get entangled in the eiderdown again? Not enough cream in your eclair? Hmmm... or did you have to talk to all your friends for so long that you didn't have time to perm your ears?"*

Guest: *"When I pay for a view, I expect something more interesting than that."*
Basil: *"But that is Torquay, madam."*
Guest: *"Well it's not good enough."*
Basil: *"Well may I ask what you expected to see out of a Torquay hotel bedroom window? Sydney Opera House perhaps? The Hanging Gardens of Babylon? Herds of wildebeest sweeping majestically across the plain..."*

Basil to Sybil: *"Can't we get you on Mastermind, Sybil? Next contestant - Sybil Fawlty from Torquay. Special subject - the bleedin' obvious."*

The Golden Girls also provided us with some sparkling verbal sparring.

Blanche: *"I treat my body like a temple."*
Sophia: *"Yeah, open to everyone, day or night."*

Rose: *"I just had a thought..."*
Sophia, Dorothy, Blanche: *"Congratulations"*

Rose: *"Well, I'm here if you want to pick my brain."*
Dorothy: *"Rose, honey. Maybe we should leave it alone and let it heal."*

Blanche: *"I was once told I bore a striking resemblance to Cheryl Ladd... but my bosoms are perkier."*
Dorothy: *"Not even if you were hanging upside-down from a trapeze!"*

Mrs Brown's boys in the 2010s likewise provided us with many excellent put downs. The 'female' lead, Agnes is a grumpy old woman with a quick and vulgar temper.

Grandad: "I don't feel well."
Agnes Brown : "You are 92 years old, you are not supposed to fucking feel well."

Agnes Brown: "You've heard of Doctor Dolittle. There goes Doctor Do Fuck All."

Tennis Players

The ATP and WTA tours include obligatory post match interviews, these, along with the on court pressure, have resulted in some amusing examples of the subtle and not so subtle insult.

Martina Hingis on Amelie Mauresmo: *"She's here with her girlfriend. She's half a man already."*

Martina Hingis when asked about her rivalry with Anna Kournikova: *"What rivalry? I win all the matches."*

Serena Williams On Martina Hingis: "She just speaks her mind and you know I guess it has a little bit to do with not having a formal education"-

Anna Kournikova after losing to Lindsay Davenport *"She doesn't hit that hard, I mean there are players that hit harder like Lucic and her serve is not that big either."*
Davenport responded: *"Anna can say whatever she wants. The point is that I'm in the semis and she's in the hotel room packing."*

Hana Mandlikova, who lost to Martina Navratilova in 3 sets in the 1984 French Open SF: *"It's hard to play against a man, I mean, Martina."* –

Reporter: *"Are you still a lesbian?"*
Martina Navratilova: *"Are you still the alternative?"*

Andre: Agassi: *"My feelings are he [Yevgeny Kafelnikov] should take his prize money when he is done here and go and buy some perspective ."*

Andre Agassi on Pete Sampras *"Nobody should be ranked No 1 who looks like he just swung from a tree".*

John McEnroe to a heckler in the crowd: *"Do you have any problems other than that you're unemployed and a moron and a dork?"*

John McEnroe to an official: *"Did you win a lottery to be a linesman?"*

John McEnroe to an official: *"You can't see as well as these fucking flowers - and they're fucking plastic."*

Nick Kyrgios to Stan Wawrikna: *"Kokkinakis banged your girlfriend, sorry to tell you that mate."*

Maria Sharapova: *"I'm not the next Anna Kournikova — I want to win matches."*

Andy Roddick *"Stay in school kids or you'll end up being an umpire."*

Andy Roddick to an umpire: *"Have you heard about that part of a body called a spine? Get one."*

Alex Ramsey: *"Michael Chang has all the fire and passion of a public service announcement."*

Richard Krajicek: *"80 per cent of the top 100 women are fat pigs who don't deserve equal pay".*

He later 'apologised'

Richard Krajicek: *"What I meant to say was that only 75 per cent are fat pigs.".*

Kate Adie: *"The three most depressing words in the English Language: 'Come on Tim'".*

Linda Smith: *"Tim Henman is so anonymous. He's like a human form of beige."*

Martina Navratilova: *"Sure I know where the press room is - I just look for where they throw the dog meat."*

Matthew Norman: *"Roger Federer is an immeasurably more charming human being than McEnroe. Then again, so was Pol Pot."*

Chris Evert on Jimmy Connors: *" I remember when Jimmy and I went into confession and he came out half an hour later and I said 'How did it go?' He said 'I wasn't finished and the Priest said come back next Sunday."*

Chris Evert: *"Sandra Cechnini is the sort of player that when you lose to her, you know you must have beaten yourself.*

Football and footballers

Whilst not famed for their intelligence, football players and managers have still provided some sharp tongued rhetoric that is great to reflect on.

George Best on David Beckham: *"He can't kick with his left foot, he can't head, he can't tackle, and he doesn't score many goals. Apart from that, he's all right."*

Brian Clough: *"The players haven't got enough heart to fill a Thimble."*

Martin O'Neill to Brian Clough: *"Why have I been dropped to the second team?"*
Clough: *"Because Martin, you are much too good for my third team."*

Giovanni Trapattoni when asked if he would be selecting Paolo Di Canio: *"Only if there's an outbreak of bubonic plague."*

Tommy Docherty: *"John Barnes's problem is that he gets injured appearing on A Question of Sport."*

Liverpool manager Bill Shankly: *"When I have got nothing better to do I look down the table to see how Everton are getting along."*

Dave Jones on Carlton Palmer: *"He covers every blade of grass, but that's only because his first touch is crap."*

Jose Mourhinho to Lionel Messi: *"How do you say cheating in Catalan?"*

Liam Gallagher on Alex Ferguson: *"He's a top manager and that but he looks like a dustbin man."*

Mark McGhee on Barry Fry *"His management style seems to be based on the chaos theory."*

Harry Redknapp: *"Harston's got more previous than Jack the Ripper."*

George best on Paul Gascoigne: *"Paul Gascoigne wears a number 10 jersey. I thought it was his position but it turns out to be his IQ."*

Alan Birchenall: *"If brains were chocolate, Robbie Savage wouldn't have enough to fill a smartie."*

Ray Clemence to Bill Shankly after conceding a goal: *"Sorry boss, I forgot to close my legs*
Shankly: *No, your mother should have.*

Freddy Shepherd on Alan Shearer: *"he's boring isn't he? We call him Mary Poppins."*

Harry Rednap on Iain Dowie: *"Judging by the shape of his face, he must have headed a lot of goals."*

Tommy Docherty on Lorenzo Amoruso: *"Somebody compared him to Billy McNiel, but I don't remember Billy McNiel being crap."*

Steve Claridge: *"Someone said you could write Barry Fry's knowledge of tactics on a stamp. You'd need to fold the stamp in half."*

Alex Fergusson on Arsene Wenger: *"Old vinegar face."*

Alex fergusson on Eric Cantona: *"he couldn't tackle a fish supper."*

Brian Clough: *"Trevor Bookings floats like a butterfly and stings like one."*

Brian Clough: *"Gary Megson couldn't trap a landmine."*

Brian Clough to Eddie Gray: *"If you were a horse you would have been shot."*

Brian Clough on John Robertson: *"He didn't look anything like a professional athlete when I first clapped eyes on him. In fact, there were times when he barely resembled a member of the human race."*

Brian Clough *"If Jimmy Hill can find a ground where he scored a league goal, I'll meet him there."*

Cris Freddi: *"Brian Clough's record speaks for itself, if it can get a word in."*

Rodney Marsh: *"Comparing Gascoigne to Pele is like comparing Rolf Harris to Rembrant."*

Tommy Docherty: *"Tom Hateley had it all! The only thing he lacked was ability."*

Tommy Docherty on Ray Wilkins: *"He can't run, can't tackle and can't head a ball. The only time he goes forward is to toss the coin."*

Gary Lineker on Sven Goran Eriksson *"He has a lot of forhead."*

Michael Owen: *"@piersmorgan Please, I beg you, bore off and stop talking about football. Tweet about things you know. Newspapers, Cakes, Doughnuts etc."*

Boxing

Perhaps the repeated blows to the head account for why boxers say some of the most outrageous things about their competitors.

Muhammad Ali: *"Joe Frazier is so ugly he should donate his face to the US Bureau of Wildlife."*

Micky Duff on Chris Eubank: *"as genuine as a 3 dollar bill."*

Ken Norton: *"My wife just had a baby."*
Joe Frazier: *"Congratulations, whose baby was it?"*

David Hayne on his scheduled fight with Audley Harrison: *"It's going to be as one sided as gang rape."*

Muhammad Ali on Joe Frazier: *"Frazier has two chances. Slim and none. And slim just left town."*

Willie Pep, when asked by a previous opponent if he recognised him: *"Lie down so I can recognise you."*

Marvin Hagler to James Tillis: *"Congratulations, you've got a great future behind you."*

Muhammad Ali: *"Joe Frazier is so ugly that when he cries, the tears turn around and go down the back of his head."*

Muhammad Ali: *"I'll beat him so bad, he'll need a shoehorn to put his hat on"*

Muhammad Ali: *"I've seen George Foreman shadow boxing and the shadow won."*

George Foreman: *"Buster Douglas is a nice guy but he is a bore. His poster could put people to sleep."*

Ray Gandolfo on Muhammad Ali: *"He now floats like an anchor and stings like a moth."*

Rocky Graziano: *"Me and Jake LaMotta grew up in the same neighbourhood. You want to know how popular Jake was? When we played hide and seek, nobody ever looked for LaMotta."*

Herby Hide on Audley Harrison: *"He's not strong enough to smash an egg with a baseball bat."*

Larry Holmes on Rocky Marciano: *"he couldn't carry my jock strap."*

Tommy Morrison on George Foreman: *"I have an advantage in this fight. I have only one chin to expose."*

Cricket

Lest we forget Cricket – the sport of the original sledgers

Mark Waugh: *"Look who it is. Mate, what are you doing here? There's no way you're good enough to play for England."*
James Ormond: *"Maybe not, but at least I'm the best player in my family."*

Glenn McGrath: *"Oi, Brandes, why are you so fat?",*
Eddo Brandes: *"because every time I sleep with your wife, she gives me a biscuit."*

Rick Broadbent on Merv Hughes: *"He always appeared to be wearing a tumble-dried ferret on his top lip."*

Fan to Phil Tuftnell: *"Oi Tuftnell, lend us your brain we are building an idiot."*

Glenn McGrath: *"Athers, it would help if you got rid of the shit at the end of your bat."*
Michael Atherton - *looks at the bottom of his bat.*
Glenn McGrath: *"No, No, the other end."*

Merv Hughes to Graham Gooch: *"I'll get you a fucking piano you Pommie poofta. Let's see if you can play that."*

Rodney Marsh: *"So how's your wife and my kids?"*
Ian Botham: *"The wife's fine - the kids are retarded."*

Merv Hughes: *"You can't fucking bat."*
Robin Smith hits Hughes for four.
Smith: *"Hey Merv, we make a fine pair. I can't fucking bat and you can't fucking bowl."*

4 years later….

Hughes: *"It's four years since I bowled to you and you haven't improved"*
Smith hits Hughes for four.

Smith: *"Neither have you."*

Dennis Lille: *"Geoffery Boycott is the only fellow I have ever met who fell in love with himself at a young age and has remained faithful ever since."*

Warne: *"I have been waiting 2 years for another chance to humiliate you."*
Cullinan: *"looks like you spent it eating."*

Talk Show Hosts

During the 1990s a new breed of interviewer emerged, they kind that did not treat their guests with reverence and vied to be the most insulting they could be.

Mrs. Merton: to Germaine Greer: *"You were a right old slapper in the seventies, weren't you?"*

Mrs. Merton to Debbie McGee: *"What was it that first attracted you to millionaire Paul Daniels?"*

Mrs. Merton to Debbie McGee: *"I think of you both as our version of David Copperfield and Claudia Schiffer, but you know, on a lower budget"*

Mrs. Merton to Barbara Windsor *"That's what I love about you Barbara, you're one of us... You're like a big film star, but you're still common as muck!"*

Mrs. Merton to Bernard Manning: *"I remember going to your club once and I laughed and laughed ... It was the night it burned down."*

Mrs Merton to Bernard Manning *"Who do you vote for now Hitler's dead?"*

Dennis Pennis to Joan Collins *: "You look like a million lire! ....Which is about 25 quid. About the price of a cup of coffee around this part of the world"*

Dennis Pennis: to Arnold Schwarzenegger: *"Arnold, you're one of Hollywood's biggest names, man! Seventeen letters!"*

Dennis Pennis to Kenneth Clarke: *"It's such a shame you didn't become leader, I look at you and I think what a waste... What a massive waist!"*

Dennis Pennis to Demi Moore: *"Are there any circumstances, if it wasn't gratuitous and it was tastefully done, would consider keeping your clothes on in a movie?"*

Dennis Pennis to Sharon Stone: *"Sharon, hi. Can you clear something up for us? In the BBC there's rumours going around that you were tricked into that infamous sequence in Basic Instinct."*
Sharon Stone: "I'm afraid that's a thing of the past."
Dennis Pennis: "Because from where I was, you looked fully debriefed."

Dennis Pennis to Pierce Brosnan: *" I gotta tell ya, I saw Goldeneye, I was glued to my seat. Otherwise I would have left!"*

Dennis Pennis to Cher: *" Has anyone told you you're really beautiful... and meant it?"*

Dennis Pennis: *"Michael, I understand you have nine toilets. Is that right, you have nine toilets?"*
Michael Winner: *"I have nine toilets, but I didn't bring any of them with me."*
Dennis Pennis: *"So you obviously make a lot more crap than people give you credit for."*

Dennis Pennis: "Do you think it's about time you got awarded with a sort of, the honours list, you know the Queen's honour's list? You should be Michael Winner O.B.E.S.E."
Michael Winner: "Oh, thank God, you should be in charge!"

Ali G : *"So now, Beckham, let's talk about fashion. We has all seen pictures of you wearing clothes that was well embarrassing and make you a proper laughing stock! What's the name of that dress that you wore?"*
David Beckham : *"Sarong."*
Ali G: *"Yeah I know it was so wrong."*

Ali G to David Beckham : *"Now, just because its Comic Relief doesn't mean you can speak in a silly voice."*

Ali G to Victoria Beckham: *"So tell me, does Brooklyn (2 year old son) like your music, or is he getting a bit old for it now?"*

Ali G to David and Victoria Beckham : *"Do you want him [their son] to grow up and be a footballer like his dad, or a singer like...Mariah Carey?"*

Clive Anderson to Jeffery Archer *"Is there no beginning to you talents?"*

Barry Gibb: "Before we were the Bee Gees we were Les Tossers
Clive Anderson: "You will always be tossers to me."

Clive Anderson: *"You're hit writers aren't you? I think that's the word anyway."*
Barry Gibb: *"That's the nice word."*
Clive Anderson: *"We are one letter short."*

Barry Gibb: "We had a hit called don't forget to remember."
Clive Anderson: "I've forgotten that one."

**Chelsea Handler*:* "You're a big star in England, like a Kim Kardashian right? Why don't you explain to people what you do?"
Jordan: "God, well how long have you got?"
Chelsea Handler: "Six minutes."

Chelsea Handler: *"Is your boyfriend a celebrity?*
Jordan: *"Well he might be now he is seen with me*
Chelsea Handler: *"Well I am sure you will take him right to the middle."*

Chelsea Handler to Jordan: " Well good luck in all your endeavours, 33 books is pretty impressive, even if they are children's books."

Chelsea Handler: *"The way you're looking at me makes me want to cover up my vagina."*
Russell Brand: *"madam, if i had rubber gloves I'd do it for you."*

Chelsea Handler to Noel Fielding: *"I think you look cute, I mean you look like you are on drugs but you look adorable."*

Chelsea Handler: "Have you guys heard of Nicaragua."
Noel Fielding: "Well yeah, because we were schooled in England."

Kumars at no 42 to Phil Collins after he won an academy award: "*When they read your name out, were you as surprised as everyone else?*"

Talent shows

Of course, Simon Cowell could not be missed from any compendium of insults. His comments to contestants on programmes such as X Factor and American idol have made headlines.

"If your lifeguard duties were as good as your singing, a lot of people would be drowning."

"If you would be singing like this two thousand years ago, people would have stoned you."

"It was a bit like ordering a hamburger, and only getting the bun."

"You have the personality of a handle."

"My advice would be if you want to pursue a career in the music business, don't."

"It would be like coaching a one-legged man to win the 100 meter sprint. I may be a great coach, but if you haven't got it, you haven't got it."

"Oh, gosh, where do I start? I mean I'm not being rude but you look like the Incredible Hulk's wife."

"It was a little bit like a Chihuahua trying to be a tiger."

"Let me throw a mathematical dilemma at you – there's 500 left, well how come the odds of you winning are a million to one?"

Cowell however has not been the only judge to engage in some amusing verbal sparring with contestants.

Sharon Osbourne to Rebecca Loos : *"If you make it through, you should try wearing knickers tomorrow, because they will help warm your voice up a bit."*

And again to the unfortunate Miss. Loos

"How about going down... you sound like you have something in the back of your throat."

Gary Barlow was also capable of driving in the knife.

"Things mature nicely like a red wine or a cheese. You've matured like a bad curry."

And this to a Russian contestant

"It's ironic that most of the words in Russian end in off."

Nigel Lythgoe to Kym Marsh: *"Christmas may be gone, but I see the goose is still fat."*

However, some of the best moments have come when the judges turned on each other.

Louie Walsh to Sharon Osbourne: *"Have you been taking Ozzy's drugs?"*

Louie Walsh to Danni Minogue: *"How would you know? You've never had a hit."*

Sharon Osbourne on Danni Minnogue: *"She's like a spoon with hair."*

Sharon Osbourne on Danni Minnogue: *"She's as dim as a bulb in a power cut. Fucking useless."*

Gary Barlow to Tulisa : *"Tulisa, I don't know what's offended me more - what you said or the fag ash breath."*

Whilst I accept that calling the Eurovision song contest a 'talent show' may well be a bridge too far, the entries often allow for some amusing quips from the likes of Terry Wogan and Graham Norton

Graham Norton:

"They're dressed like posh hospital workers from the future."

"If you've just joined us and thought, 'Ooh, Denise van Outen's let herself go', no, that's Cascada representing Germany"

"Her outfit does involve some roadkill. I fear some Georgian crows were harmed in the making of this act."

"Small children and pets should probably move from the room. Here's Cezar, proving that just because you can do something, doesn't mean you should."

"This will put fear into your heart – she's a devoted experimental jazz musician. She can do extraordinary things with her voice…not pleasant things but extraordinary."

"It's obviously dress-down Saturday in Denmark."

"To add to the fun, she's dressed as a novelty toilet brush."

"At points you may think you had a bad oyster, but it's actually choreographed."

"The song is called "N'oubliez pas', which means 'don't forget.' Sadly, I think we will."

"He says he did something awful, it may be this song."

Terry Wogan

Describing the hosts: *"Doctor Death and the Tooth Fairy,"*

"Who knows what hellish future lies ahead? ... Actually, I do. I've seen the rehearsals,"

"Thank God we've all had a few drinks - if anyone can kill a crowd these two can!"

"And to sing for Cyprus, and wearing his mother's curtains - Konstaninos!"

"But it's the same song the French have been singing since they hung the washing out on the Maginot Line."

"Another of these plain girls that Eurovision is afflicted with this year"

"You've got four dancers, for whom modern dance stopped about 30 years ago."

"It's during that kind of song that you begin to notice the set a bit more"

"Keep an eye on this fella, I don't think he's the full shilling!"

"When you pick a boy band usually, you pick them for their good looks. But the Russians appear to have gone to the other extreme"

"Old kids on the block!"

The Music business

Musicians have often been famed for their rivalries, their throwing of shade and their tempestuous natures, the advent of social media has made it all the better.

Liam Gallagher on Victoria Beckham's autobiography: *"She can't even chew gum and walk in a straight line at the same time, let alone write a book."*

Noel Gallagher: *"Take That's Howard Donald said in a documentary that he hears voices at night willing him to fail. To fail at what? You don't do anything Howard."*

Prince *"Michael Jackson's album was called Bad because there wasn't enough room on the sleeve for Pathetic."*

Madonna to Elton John: *"The easiest way for you to lose 10 pounds is just to take off your wig."*

Emma Jones on Lily Allen: *"Lily Alen has got something of the street about her, she has a bit of a diner lady face."*

Richey Edwards: *"You could go to any Levellers concert and stand in the middle and shout 'Jeremy!'. 75% of the audience would turn around."*

Alan McGee: *"Coldplay are the dictionary definition of corporate rock. EMI should have signed Otis the Ardvark instead. At least he only sucks his thumb and not corporate cock."*

Fan to Cher: *"How did you celebrate Madonna's birthday?"*
Cher: *"I got a colonic."*

Noel Gallagher: *"I did drugs for 18 years and I never got that bad as to say 'You know what? I think the Kaiser Chiefs are brilliant."*

Noel Gallagher: *"I would rather drink petrol straight from the nozel in a garage that listen to an interview with Alex Turner from the Arctic Monkies."*

Nick Cave: *"I am forever near a stereo saying 'What the fuck is this garbage?' The answer is always the Red Hot Chilli Peppers."*

Interviewer: *"What do you think about Mariah Carey?"*
Whitney Houston: *"I don't think about her."*

Boy George on Elton John: *"All that money and he's still got hair like a fucking dinner lady."*

Boy George: *"I heard Michael Jackson is moving to France. For the first time my sympathies are with the French people."*

Boy George: *"Prince looks like a dwarf who's been dipped in a bucket of pubic hair."*

Paul Young on Boy George: *"Boy George reminds me of a aubergine, all shiny and plump."*

Elton John on Keith Richards: *"It's like a monkey with arthritis, trying to go onstage and look young."*

Elvis Costello: *"Morrisey writes wonderful song titles, but sadly he often forgets to write the songs."*

Britt Ekland on ex Rod Stewart: *"He was so mean it hurt him to go to the bathroom."*

Joan Rivers: "Mick Jagger could French-kiss a moose. He has child-bearing lips."

Tulisa to Alan Sugar: *"You look like an ugly old hobbit. Stop tweeting me & go & find some happiness! It's embarrassing u miserable old man."*

James Arthur to Frankie Boyle: Tweet " Poor old man making yet more shit jokes about X Factor because he knows that's the only way he can get attention anymore #Prat."
Frankie Boyle's reply: *"I think if I wanted attention I'd sing covers on a talent show inked up like a schooldesk in a remedial class."*

What better way to cause a commotion than boy band wars?

Zayn Malik: *"@MaxTheWanted I'm not sure why your still talking to me mate conversation ended when I called you a geek."*
Max *"@zaynmalik that's not very nice. I was just starting to like you and your RnB hits."*
Tom: *"@zaynmalik @maxthewanted I think "1 stripes" got his knickers in a twist bro."*
Zayn *"@TomTheWanted mate if I had a face like yours my hair would be the last thing I'd worry about :)."*

Noel Gallagher: *"Just because you sell lots of records doesn't mean to say you are any good. Look at Phil Collins."*

Mariah Carey on Madonna: *"I was a fan of hers when she was popular."*

Noel Gallagher on Jack White: *"He looks like Zorro on doughnuts."*

David Coverdale on Madonna: *"I have seen Madonna up close. Neither the music nor the image inspire my loins."*

Katy Perry on Mariah Carey: *"She is fantastic... for a throw back."*

Whitney Houston on Madonna: *"The high priestess of tack."*

Noel Gallagher on Liam Gallagher: *"He's gone to the zoo. The monkeys are bringing their kids to look at him."*

Noel Gallagher: *"Kylie Minogue is just a demonic little idiot as far as I am concerned."*

50 Cent on Kanye West: *"It's not possible for Kanye to beat me. It's like the teddy bear versus the gorilla."*

Katy Perry on pulling away from a kiss with Miley Cyrus: *"God knows where that tongue has been."*

Liam Gallagher on Robbie Williams: *"You mean that fat dancer from Take That."*

Bette Midler on Madonna: *"The only thing Madonna will ever do like a virgin is give birth on a stable floor."*

Perez Hilton tweeted Cher about a comment made by Piers Morgan on Madonna: *"@cher Piers said @Madonna shouldn't be wearing fishnets and revealing costumes because she's 56. I said he's ageist and sexist!"* **Cher: "***If Piers doesn't want to see fishnets on an old Diva's legs, He shouldn't wear them."*

Prince Philip to Tom Jones: *"What do you gargle with, pebbles?"*.

Oscar Levant to George Gershwin: *"Play us a medley of your hit."*

Drake Bell: *"I really wish Beiber Fever were fatal."*

Mariah Carey on Jennifer Lopez: *"I would rather be onstage with a pig."*

Christian Aguilera on Kelly Osbourne: *"Oh Lord, I didn't realise it was still Halloween."*

Pete Burns on Lionel Richie: *"He's got a chin like an ironing board."*

Simon Cowell to Jamelia: *"My advice would be to have a second hit and then you can have an opinion."*

Amanda Bynes to Rhianna: *"Chris brown beat you because you're not pretty enough."*
Rhianna: *"You see what happens when they cancel therapy."*

Chris Brown: *"HAPPY VALENTINES DAY to all the beautiful women around the world.. Know that you are loved and appreciated !! God bless."*
Lindsay Ellis *"@chrisbrown awww I bet you say that to all the victims."*

Singer James Blunt is perhaps the master of dealing with abusive fans, his twitter feed is genuinely hilarious.

@Alif_novaldi: Fuck you James blunt
@JamesBlunt *"I'm sorry, but you'll have to get to the back of the queue. RT"*

@hettjones: James Blunt just has an annoying face and a highly irritating voice
@JamesBlunt: and no mortgage

@anadinskywalker: my grandma just called james blunt a queer
@JamesBlunt: Only coz I turned her down

@ChrisPaJones: Why does James Blunt have a new album and why would people want that?
@JamesBlunt: I am guessing you are a philiosopher.

In reply to a woman who insinuated she wanted to punch him
@JamesBlunt: you look more like a slapper than a puncher.

@Raghallaigh: @JamesBlunt Holy cunting christ your music makes me want to cave my own skull in with a hammer!
@JamesBlunt: Be my guest

@_idkmatilda: has James blunt done anything other than that one song in his whole career
@JamesBlunt: Just that and a few super models.

@_tusekile: James blunt is one ugly mother fucker
@JamesBlunt: and how is your modelling career going?

@TroyJosephDavis: no one really likes James Blunt right?
@JamesBlunt: Yeah I bought those 20 million albums myself.

@DJWagstaff11: Day couldnt get any worse than @JamesBlunt coming on the radio at work... #notbeautiful
@JamesBlunt: My Bad. Missed my hanky.

@garymoody65: @JamesBlunt why you only got 200k followers?
@JamesBlunt: Jesus only needed 12.

@lizziea1: I want to kick James Blunt... repeatedly ... I don't know why.
@JamesBlunt: Easy spelling mistake as K and L are right beside each other

@MigsterMMA: Jesus christ, James Blunt's got a new album out. Is there anything else that can go wrong?
@JamesBlunt: Yes. He could start tweeting you

@NME: Noel Gallagher says songs about his own life would be 'more boring than James Blunt'
@JamesBlunt: For once, I agree with him.

@supermarton: James Blunt es lo peor que le ha pasado a la humanidad desde Hitler
@JamesBlunt: I am guessing this is not good.

@IndyMusic: Noel Gallagher says he cannot live in a world where Ed Sheeran sells out Wembley Stadium.
@JamesBlunt: Time to legalise assisted dying.

@Thomasemaan: Just realized how short James Blunt is !!!
@JamesBlunt: It's only half way in.

@sassyfalahee: omfg james blunt is on the tv downstairs can this day get any worse!
@JamesBlunt: Coming upstairs now.

@vivadasilvas: James Blunt. What a twat he is.
@JamesBlunt: Like Yoda you speak.

@gravedads: I thought James Blunt died
@JamesBlunt: I did but you will never guess what happened on the third day.

@GaryLineker James Blunt sounds a bit too posh to me to be a pop star.
@James Blunt: Interesting, what other sorts of prejudice are you into?

@jamesBlunt: My real name is James Blount, but I changed it as people teased me that it rhymed with 'count'.

@Doda127: Do you have to be a knob for @JamesBlunt to respond?
@JamesBlunt: Yes

@Lilley_padwar: James Blunt rhymes with cunt, just saying.
@jamesBlunt: Says Laura Lilley, who's last name rhymes with cock.

@Buizel0418: My mom hates James Blunt. xD
@JamesBlunt: Because I wont pay the child support

@AmirM96: why have I got James Blunt stuck in my head this morning
@JamesBlunt: My bad. Tea bagging gone wrong.

@something_robot: Waking up with James Blunt stuck in your head. Nowt worse.
@jamesBlunt. Worse for me as there's nothing else in here.

Graffiti

Even Graffiti can provide us with examples of quick put downs and checks on large egos.

Original	"Don't hate me because I am beautiful, hate me because I did your dad"
Reply	"Go home Mum, you're drunk"
Original	"I am 9 inches, do you want me?"
Reply	"It depends how big your penis is."
Sign	"This year, thousands of men will die from stubbornness."
Graffiti	"No we wont"
Sign	"This door is alarmed."
Graffiti	"What startled it?"
Sign	"Bill posters will be prosecuted."
Graffiti	"Bill Posters is an innocent man."
Original	"Satin rules." Over picture of a pentagram
Reply	"Well…. It is a nice fabric and all but I don't know if it rules."
Original	"You are walking into an awful place." (Above toilet door)
Reply	"Worse than Sheffield?"
Original	"A guy who writes lame graffiti in permanent ink on bathroom walls is selfish and uninteresting and annoys everyone around him. We all live here, now do your fucking part to keep this place clean and cut that shit out mmmmokay."
Reply	"Disregard that I suck cock." Added below
Original	"Stop the idea of societies mutated self image. We are all beautiful!!!
Reply	"Bet a fat girl wrote this."

Original	"Uk if full n we cant keep letting imirgrants in all the time taking are jobs and house and are benefits. Why dont we do nothing about it and keep them out specially Poles and Lifuanians. UK FULL UK FULL UK FULL UK FULL UK FULL UK FULL UK FULL UK FULL UK FULL UK FULL UK FULL UK FULL UK FULLUK FULL UK FULL UK FULL UK FULL UK FULL UK FULLUK FULL UK FULL UK FULL UK FULL UK FULL UK FULLUK FULL UK FULL UK FULL UK FULL UK FULL UK FULL UK FULLWHY WE GIVING EM ARE JOBS WHY WE GIVING THEM ARE JOBSWHY WE GIVING EM ARE JOBS WHY WE GIVING THEM ARE JOBS WHY WE GIVING EM ARE JOBS WHY WE GIVING THEM ARE JOBS WHY WE GIVING EM ARE JOBS WHY WE GIVING THEM ARE JOBS WHY WE GIVING EM ARE JOBS WHY WE GIVING THEM ARE JOBS WHY WE GIVING EM ARE JOBS WHY WE GIVING THEM ARE JOBS"
REPLY	" Perhaps it is because we can spell, punctuate and evidently have much shorter toilet breaks."
Original	My Dick is hard
Reply	To find?

The Movies

Planes, Trains and Automobiles: *"If I wanted a joke, I'd follow you into the John and watch you take a leak"*

Stand By Me: *"Did your mother have any children that lived?"*

The Witches of Eastwick: *"You are physically repulsive, intellectually retarded, you're morally reprehensible, vulgar, insensitive, selfish, stupid, you have no taste, a lousy sense of humour and you smell. You're not even interesting enough to make me sick."*

The Breakfast Club: *"Does Barry Manilow know that you raid his wardrobe?"*

Outrageous Fortunes:
Sandy: Oh, my... that kind of evening, huh?
Lauren: Well, not the kind you're used to; no money changed hands!

Con Air: *"You're somewhere between a cockroach and that white stuff that accumulates at the corner of your mouth when you're really thirsty. But, in your case, I'll make an exception."*

Stand By Me: *"I'm goona rip your head off and shit down your neck."*

Gleaming the Cube: *"If my dog had a face like yours I'd shave his ass and teach him to walk backwards."*

Full Metal Jacket: *"It looks to me like the best part of you ran down the crack of your mama's ass and ended up as a brown stain on the mattress."*

Casablanca:
UGARTE: "You despise me, don't you?"
RICK: "If I gave you any thought I probably would."

Duck Soup: *"I can see you right now in the kitchen, bending over a hot stove. But I can't see the stove."*

Dodgeball: *"Holy hell, son, you're about as useful as a cock-flavored lollipop!"*

Blazing Saddles: *"Shut up you Teutonic twat."*

Parenthood: *"I wouldn't live with you if the world were flooded wih piss and you lived in a tree."*

Monty Python and the Holy Grail: *"I fart in your general direction. Your mother was a hamster and your father smelt of elderberries."*

Stand By Me:
Teddy: Okay, you guys can go around if you want. I'm crossing here. And while you guys are dragging your candy asses half way across the state and back, I'll be waiting on the other side, relaxing with my thoughts.
Gordie: You use your left hand or right hand to do that?

Raging Bull: *"You punch like you take it up arse."*

Roxanne: *"Is that your nose, or did someone park on your face?"*

Get Carter: *"You know, I'd almost forgotten what your eyes looked like. Still the same. Piss holes in the snow."*

The Ref: *"You know what, Mom, you know what I'm going to get you next Christmas? A big wooden cross, so every time you feel unappreciated for all your sacrifices, you can climb on up and nail yourself to it."*

Comedians

Rufus Hound about a heckler: *"Can we get some crayons and a menu for this guy to colour please."*

Anonymous to heckler: *"Excuse me, I'm trying to work here. How would you like it if I started yelling down the alley while you're giving blow jobs to transsexuals?"*

Jimmy Carr to a heckler: *"If you want my comeback you will have to scrape it off your mum's teeth."*

Jack Dee to a heckler: *"Well, it's a night out for him, isn't it? And for his family it's a night off."*

John Cooper Clarke to a heckler: *"Your bus leaves in 10 minutes... Be under it."*

Russell Kane to a heckler: *"Why don't you go into a corner and finish evolving."*

Jasper Carrot to a heckler: *"Sit back in your chair and I'll plug it in."*

Heckler: *"I met you at medical school."*
Frank Skinner: *"Ah yes, you were the one in the jar."*

Ian Hislop: *"He looked like King Edward, the potatoe not the monarch."*

Joan Rivers: *"I was hoping maybe Gwyneth Paltrow was starting a stupid trend by naming her child after her favourite food…. Christina Aguilera's next kid should be called Potato."*

Joan Rivers: *"You want to get Cindy Crawford confused? Ask her to spell 'mom' backwards."*

Chelsea Handler on the Jonas brothers: *"Until they penetrate who knows what side of the see-saw they sit on."*

Chelsea Handler on Angelina Jolie and her adopted son: "He probably thought he was scoring the biggest deal of his lifetime, getting adopted by this famous movie star who was going to rescue him from his third-world Cambodia, only to find out she was going to take him to every other third-world country in the world. He's probably like, 'When are we going to get to Malibu?"

Jonathan Ross: "Some people are a bit unkind about some of the female tennis players, but I've met Lindsay Davenport and he's a lovely feller."

Chelsea Handler: "I just heard Nick Cannon is starting a comedy tour. Who's going to do the comedy?"

Nick Cannon: "@chelseahandler is like the new @joanrivers just without the funny and more plastic surgery."

Johnny Carson on Don Rickles: "I have seen Don entertain fifty times and I've always enjoyed his joke."

Stephen Fry: "What's the commonest material in the world?"
Clive Anderson: "Jim Davidson's."

Frankie Boyle: "Remember tonight isn't all about comedy. Here's Ben Elton."

Clive James: " Joan Rivers's face hasn't just had a lift, it's taken the elevator all the way to the top floor without stopping."

Joan Rivers: "Lindsay Lohan said she wouldn't mind being under oath because she thought Oath was a Norwegian ski instructor."

Joan Rivers: "I said Justin Bieber looked like a little lesbian — and I stand by it: He's the daughter Cher wishes she'd had."

Joan Rivers: "Is Elizabeth Taylor fat? Her favorite food is seconds,"

Paul Merton: "It has just been revealed that Brian Blessed's wife has been found in a cellar beneath their house. The cellar was completely sound proof. The twist is she built it herself."

Angus Deayton: "Apparently the Queen also refers to John Prescott as "Two Jags".
Paul Merton: "That's rich coming from Elizabeth "Six castles" Windsor!"

Piers Morgan: *"Is the answer jam? I only said that because last week Eddie Izzard said that and you roared with laughter, as if it was hilarious. Just thought I'd say it."*
Ian Hislop: *"People like him."*

Clive Anderson: *"Do you still live in Islington as well, Boris?"*
Boris Johnson: *"Partly, yes."*
Paul Merton: *"I don't think you live on the planet Earth, never mind Islington!"*

Jonathan Ross on Heather Mills: *"She's a fucking liar…. I wouldn't be surprised if we found out she's actually got 2 legs."*

Jonathan Ross *"Liz Hurley longs for the day when people stop pointing cameras at her. Speaking as someone who has seen all her films, I couldn't agree more."*

Frankie Boyle: *"@piersmorgan If you died tomorrow they could cater your funeral with a packet of Monster Munch."*

Frankie Boyle: *"To be fair to James Arthur, he only has a problem with 1D because they remind him of his GCSE results."*

Clive James: "Beyoncé and pathos are strangers. Amy Winehouse and pathos are flatmates, and you should see the kitchen."

Clive James on Barbara Cartland: *"Twin miracles of mascara, her eyes looked like the corpses of two small crows that had crashed into a chalk cliff."*

Clive James on Marilyn Monroe: *"So minimally gifted as to be almost unemployable"*

Clive James on George W Bush *"Every sentence he manages to utter scatters its component parts like pond water from a verb chasing its own tail."*

Clive James on Murray Walker: *"Even in moments of tranquillity, Murray Walker sounds like a man whose trousers are on fire"*

Clive James on Margaret Thatcher: *"She sounded like the Book of Revelations read out over a railway station public address system by a headmistress of a certain age wearing calico knickers."*

Internet chatrooms

Go into any internet chat room on any emotive subject, gun control, the death penalty, abortion, even Justin Bieber and watch the sparks fly. Even facebook allows us to view the wit and oratory skills of others.

Have you considered putting down the crack pipe before you post?

Somewhere out there a tree is producing oxygen tirelessly so you can breath

Shut up, you'll never be the man your mother is.

The last time I saw a face like yours I fed it a banana.

I refuse to have a battle of wits with an unarmed opponent.

Maybe if you ate some of that makeup you could be pretty on the inside.

Hey, you have something on your chin... no, the 3rd one down

Two wrongs don't make a right, take your parents as an example.

I'll see you in my dreams - if I eat too much cheese

I could eat a bowl of alphabet soup and shit out a more astute and logical argument than that

Any similarity between you and a human is purely coincidental!

I'd like to give you a going away present but you have to do your part first.

Are you always so stupid or is today a special occasion?

As an outsider, what do you think of the human race?

Nice shirt – is it designer……… outlet?

They say what you don't know can't hurt you so you must be invulnerable.

I see you were so impressed with your first chin that you added two more

Your family tree must be a cactus because everybody on it is a prick.

I'm not saying I hate you, but I would unplug your life support to charge my phone.

I have had better conversations with PPI cold callers.

Well I could agree with you, but then we'd both be wrong.

Why don't you slip into something more comfortable -- like a coma.

I have neither the time nor the crayons to explain this to you.

Girl: "I wouldn't go out with you if you were the last man on earth"
Guy: "If I was the last man on earth you wouldn't be anywhere near the front of the queue"

You're not funny, but your life, now that's a joke.

I have seen better dressed wounds than you.

Does your face qualify you for disability allowance?

I imagine your face is an effective chaperone.

Oh my God, look at you. Was anyone else hurt in the accident?

If I gave you a penny for your thoughts, I'd get change.

Girl to Bieber detractor: "You are a wanker."
Bieber detractor: "If only your father was."

I'm not saying you're fat, but it looks like you were poured into your clothes and someone forgot to say "when"

Have you had your hair cut like that to distract from your face?

Learn from your parents' mistakes - use birth control!

Guy: "Well excuse me young lady, is this seat free"
Girl: "Yes, but if you sit in it, my seat will be free instead..."

I don't know what makes you so stupid, but it really works!

You look like a before picture.

He is dark and handsome. When it's dark, he's handsome.

He is known as a miracle comic. if he's funny, it's a miracle!

You fear success, but really have nothing to worry about.

You're the reason the gene pool needs a lifeguard.

I've seen people like you, but I had to pay admission!

100,000 sperm, you were the fastest?

Are your parents siblings?

I was pro-life before I met you.

At least there's one thing good about your body. It isn't as ugly as your face!

Brains aren't everything. In fact, in your case they're nothing

Have you ladies left Cinderella at home?

You have an honest face – honest, is that your face?
If you had a white tooth, you would have a snooker set.

You are almost fastidious – you are fast and hideous.

You half look like you have an eating disorder – the binge eating half

I know you're a self-made man. It's nice of you to take the blame!

I know you're not as stupid as you look. Nobody could be!

You're quite the wit, well half on one.

Some people bring happiness wherever they go; you bring happiness whenever you go.

I would have liked to have fucked your brains out but it appears someone beat me to it"

Behind every fat woman is a beautiful woman, so could you move please?

The smartest thing ever to come out of your mouth was a penis.
I would try and see things from your perspective but I doubt there is room up your arse for both our heads.

Ok, I am attempting to be charitable, I am sure you are not dumb and that you just have bad luck when you think

Is that your face or did you neck vomit?

Looks like the fuck up fairy has visited your thinking again.

Many people haven't read your posts before, I am envious of them.

Did your mother ever regret not keeping the afterbirth instead?

Do you open the post with that nose?

If bullshit could float, you would be an Admiral

For you, evolution just happened to other people didn't it?

It's great your carers are encouraging you to share your opinions on things

Have you forgotten to take your meds today?

If shit was music, you would be an orchestra

Please tell me you don't home-school your kids

Would you like some cheese to go with that whine?

Save your breath, you will need it to blow up your girlfriend.

Fascinating as talking to you has been, I have some paint I need to watch dry now.

You must be the wingman.

"Are you being deliberately patronising?"
"Yes I am, how clever you are to notice."

You are so dense I am sure light must bend around you.

You have delusions of adequacy.

You are in great shape – shame the shape is round.

A village somewhere is missing it's idiot.

Your body is a temple, albeit the temple of doom.

Oh sweetheart - I've got a fake laugh with your name written all over it."

Girl: *"I would rather sleep with any Lad in London than you."*
Guy: *"I would rather you did too and if that didn't work, I would rather I did."*

You are so stupid you couldn't pour water from a boot with instructions written on the heel

I am certainly not flirting with you, I wouldn't even put my foot in your mouth

Do you have a pen? Well get back in it?

Someday you'll go far... and I hope you stay there.

Can you remember when I asked for your opinion? Me neither!

This facebook exchange regarding a school reunion is priceless.

Larry: WTF THAT lady was youre favourite tecaher? She a bitch cuz of her I had 2 take summer school
Teacher: Sadly, I will not be able to attend but thank you all for inviting me to the group. Larry, I am sorry you feel that way. Obviously my grammar lessons didn't stick too well.
Larry: w/ever I couldn't say it in hs so I say it now URA BITHC
Teacher: Larry, you can barely say it now. Also you could have said that in High School because "BITHC" isn't a real word. I am going to use my context clues and assume you are attempting to call me a bitch. In that case, I will point out that your facebook information lets me know that you are currently single and unemployed. Who is the bitch now?

Poster 1: "My dick is so big it goes from a-z."
Poster 2: "Look at your keyboard."

Have your children hacked your account, the previous post has all the hallmarks of a juvenile in a hurry.

You are a legend in your own lunchtime.

Are you having a nonentity crisis?

I didn't take an instant dislike to you when you arrived on this site, I should have, it would have saved time.

That's the best post I have seen on here- in the last 12 seconds.

You speak on the subject like someone who has researched it – much too briefly.

You have clearly given seconds of thought to this issue.

You are the product of the tabloids you read.

Interesting point of view – in the same way as people who think plants feel pain have interesting views.

Poster 1: *"Without the ugly in this world there would be nothing beautiful*
Poster 2: *"Thank you for your sacrifice."*

Poster 1: *"This song does stuff to me that my girlfriend can't."*
Poster 2: *"That's because the music is real, your girlfriend isn't."*

Poster 1: *"I need google in my brain and antivirus in my heart."*
Poster 2: *"and photo shop on your face."*

I don't understand what you are trying to say, I am not fluent in moron.

After meeting you, I've decided I am in favour of abortion in cases of incest.

You don't look fatter in that dress, not sure ANYTHING could make you look fatter than you do.

You say you don't know the meaning of the word failure, I imagine that's one of many words you struggle with.

Poster 1: *"The 80s called. They want their haircut back."*

Poster 2: *"The 1880s called, too. They want their joke back."*

Poster 1: *"Nice tan, I love orange, it's my favourite colour."*

Poster 2: *"Mine is brown, so I adore your teeth."*

He forgot to pay his brain bill

It's like you smell the coffee but can't locate the pot.

I love what you've done with your hair. How do you get it to come out of the nostrils like that?

Did you know they used to be called "Jumpolines" until your wife jumped on one?

A moron gave you a piece of his mind and you insist on using it.

If I had a face like yours I'd sue my parents.

She is a little giddy today, her doctor called with her colonoscopy results. They found her head.

Whatever kind of look you were going for, you missed

If Shit were music you would be an orchestra

I always defend you! The other day people were saying you were not fit to eat with pigs but I said you would manage it.

Alone: In bad company.

Interesting post – ok I exaggerate.

I thought of you today. It reminded me to take the garbage out.

Can you repeat that slowly, I don't speak twat.

Don't let your mind wander -- it's too little to be let out alone.

You are pretty as a picture, I'd love to see you hung.

No I am not gay, I'm straighter than the pole your mum dances on

It's hard to get the big picture when you have such a small screen.

I don't want to be too harsh in my response to your post, I can see it is your first attempt at literacy.

I've come across decomposed bodies that are less offensive than you are.

A guy with your IQ should have a low voice too!

Excellent attempt at banter for an amoeba

I follow you only out of morbid curiosity

Your brain waves are falling a little short of the beach today.

You look great in black – the pitch black.

You would be out of your depth in a baby bath.

Any friend of yours ... is a friend of yours.

I would advise you to ignore the standard advise about 'being yourself'

Do you liaise with other plankton before forming an opinion?

Let's play horse. I'll be the front end and you be yourself.

Her origins are so low you would have to limbo under her family tree

Would you be different if you had had enough oxygen at birth?

You're so short your hair smells like your feet.

Are you the first in your family born without a tail?

He's had a personality transplant but it rejected him.

I worship the ground that awaits you.

I'll never forget the first time we met - although I'll keep trying.

You've never been one to allow fact to influence your opinions.

I bet moonlight becomes you - total darkness even more!

Some drink from the fountain of knowledge, but you just gargled.

You have a striking face. Tell me, how many times were you struck there?

You have an inferiority complex - and it's fully justified.

You're not yourself today. I noticed the improvement immediately

You've never been outspoken; no one has ever been able to.

As a boss you are different, I like the unique hands off management style.

Your IQ is barely above brain dead.

If he had a brain he would be on the floor playing with it

General insults

Marc Savlov *"As entertaining as watching a potato bake."*

Groucho Marx *"Don't look now, but there's one too many in this room and I think it's you."*

Cynthia Heimel *"If you can't live without me, why aren't you dead already?"*

Jonathan Swift *"Fine words! I wonder where you stole them."*

Groucho Marx: *"From the moment I picked your book up until I laid it down I was convulsed with laughter. Some day I intend reading it."*

Earl Long: *"A four-hundred-dollar suit on him would look like socks on a rooster."*

Neil Simon Gee: *"what a terrific party. Later on we'll get some fluid and embalm each other."*

Eddie Cantor: *"He hasn't an enemy in the world - but all his friends hate him."*

Raymond Chandler: *"He looked as inconspicuous as a tarantula on a slice of angel food."*

Edith Massey: *"At first I thought he was walking a dog. Then I realized it was his date."*

Groucho Marx: *"Don't point that beard at me, it might go off."*

Mark Twain: *"He Had double chins all the way down to his stomach."*

Noel Coward: *"He's completely unspoiled by failure."*

Arthur Miller: *"He's liked, but he's not well liked."*

Mae West: *"His mother should have thrown him away and kept the stork."*

Groucho Marx: *"I could dance with you until the cows come home. On second thought I'd rather dance with the cows until you come home."*

Stephen Bishop: *"I feel so miserable without you, it's almost like having you here."*

Clarence Darrow: *"I have never killed a man, but I have read many obituaries with great pleasure."*

Dave Clark: *"I never liked him and I always will."*

Fred Allen: *" I like long walks, especially when they are taken by people who annoy me."*

George C. Scott: *"He had a winning smile, but everything else was a loser."*

Oliver Goldsmith: *"He makes a very handsome corpse and becomes his coffin prodigiously."*

Robert Louis Stevenson: *"I regard you with an indifference bordering on aversion."*

Wilson Mizner: *"He's a trellis for varicose veins."*

Johnny Carson: *"He's so fat, he can be his own running mate."*

Irving Brecher: *"I'll bet your father spent the first year of your life throwing rocks at the stork."*

Rupert Hughes: *"Her face was her chaperone."*

Woody Allen: *"Her figure described a set of parabolas that could cause cardiac arrest in a yak."*

Fred Allen: *"Her hat is a creation that will never go out of style. It will look ridiculous year after year."*

Pauline Kael: *"Her only flair is in her nostrils."*

Irvin S. Cobb: *"I've just learned about his illness. Let's hope it's nothing trivial."*

Charles Pierce: *"If you ever become a mother, can I have one of the puppies?"*

S. T. Coleridge: *"Her skin was white as leprosy."*

Ellen Glascow: *"In her single person she managed to produce the effect of a majority."*

Ivy Compton-Burnett: *"Pushing forty? She's hanging on for dear life."*

William Shakespeare: *"She's good, being gone."*

William Dean Howells: *"Some people stay longer in an hour than others can in a week."*

Ashleigh Brilliant: *"Sometimes I need what only you can provide: your absence."*

Joseph Stilwell: *"The higher a monkey climbs, the more you see of its behind."*

Jack E. Leonard: *"There's nothing wrong with you that reincarnation won't cure."*

Hunter S. Thompson: *"They don't hardly make 'em like him any more - but just to be on the safe side, he should be castrated anyway."*

Ashleigh Brilliant: *"We've been through so much together, and most of it was your fault."*

Milton Berle: *"Why are we honoring this man? Have we run out of human beings?"*

Jane Austen: *"You have delighted us long enough."*

Jim Samuels: *"You're a good example of why some animals eat their young."*

Gregory Ratoff: *"You're a parasite for sore eyes."*

Bob Fosse: *"She not only kept her lovely figure, she's added so much to it."*

Heinrich Heine *"She resembles the Venus de Milo: she is very old, has no teeth, and has white spots on her yellow skin."*

The lights are on but.....

The lights are on but there is no one home.

The lights have turned green but he hasn't found the biting point.

The logs are burning but the chimney is clogged.

Dinner is served but nobodies eating

The wheel is spinning but the hamster is dead

The hard drive is spinning but OS hasn't been installed.

The wind is blowing but the washing isn't getting dry

He is in the field without his catchers mitt

The whistle has sounded but they can't find the ball

Shipping has occurred but delivery hasn't.

The trigger has been pulled but the bullets aint moving.

The lighter is full but the flint is soggy

The phone is connected but they can't locate a dial tone.

The tickets are bought but the plane hasn't arrived.

She's found the oars but they don't reach the water

The bicycle works but the training wheels wobble

She has a piano but can't find a tuner

He has hit search but internet explorer is not responsing

Your mum

For many young boys growing up, the epitome of a skillful insult was a well executed comment about a friend's mother. Her weight was always a great choice of subject and below are some remembered from both my own youth and the memories of other shared on the world wide web

Your mum is so fat she has 2 watches, 1 for each time zone she's in.

Your mum is so fat she left the house in high heels and when she came back she had on flip flops.

Your Mum is so fat she sat on an iPhone and turned it into an iPad

Your mum is so fat when she stepped on the scale, the doctor said "Hey, that's my Phone Number"

Your Mum is so fat that even Dora couldn't explore her

Your Mum is so fat her blood type is Snickers.

Your mum is so fat when she goes to a restaurant she gets the group discount

Your Mum is so fat you have to grease the door frame and hold a mars bar on the other side just to get her through

Your mum is so fat she lays on the beach and greenpeace tried to push her back in the water

Your mum is so fat the only pictures you have of her are satellite pictures

Your mum is so fat, she once had a nice personality, but she ate it.

Your mum is so fat, I took a photo off her last year and it's still printing

Your mum is so fat other mums orbit her.

Your mum is so fat she went to the movies and sat next to everyone

Your mum is so fat when she wears a yellow raincoat, people said "Taxi!"

Your mum is so fat she aint got cellulite she got celluheavy

Your mum is so fat her cereal bowl comes with a life guard.

The only time your mum she burns calories is when she forgets the pie in the oven.

Your mum is so fat when she gets on the scale it says to be continued.

Your mum is so fat when she gets on the scale it says we don't do livestock.

Your mum is so fat she's got her own postal code!

Your mum is so fat, she's got more chins than a Hong Kong phonebook

Your mum is so fat she downloads cheat codes for wii fit.

Your mum is so fat, her local Chinese buffet installed speed bumps

Your mum is so fat they use the elastic in her underwear for bungee jumping

Your mum is so fat she's on the seafood diet, she sees food and she eats it

Your mum is so fat she needs a lattitude and longitude number to wipe her bum

Your mum is so fat she has to wear a elastic wedding ring

Your mum is so fat she went swimming in a black bathing suit and got mistaken for an oil spill.

Whilst insulting someone's mother's weight can be most satisfying, a good effort on the intelligence of a friend's mother is also worth a try

Your Mum is so dumb she hears it's chilly outside so she gets a bowl

Your Mum is so dumb she thinks Fleetwood Mac is a new hamburger.

Your Mum is so dumb she bought tickets to Xbox Live

Your Mum is so dumb she stood on a chair to raise her IQ.

Your Mum is so dumb she thinks menopause is a button on Skyplus

Your Mum is so dumb, first time she used a vibrator she broke her two front teeth.

Your Mum is so dumb she went to the dentist to get her Bluetooth fixed.

Your Mum is so dumb she gave birth to you on the M1 because she heard thats where accidents happen

Your Mum is so dumb when the questionnaire asked sex? She put in M F and sometimes Wednesday.

Your Mum is so dumb I mentioned that Christmas was around the corner and she went looking for it

Your Mum is so dumb she went to the library to find Facebook

Your Mum is so dumb she got fired from a blow job

Your Mum is so dumb, she failed a survey.

Your Mum is so dumb you have to dig for her IQ!

Your Mum is so dumb she sold her car for petrol money!

Your mum is so dumb the only letters in the alphabet she knows are K.F.C.

Your Mum is so dumb she thinks a quarterback is a refund!

Your Mum is so dumb she thought TuPac Shakur was a Jewish holiday

Your Mum is so dumb she sent me a fax with a stamp on it

Your Mum is so dumb she tried to put M&M's in alphabetical order

Your Mum is so dumb she spent 20 minutes looking at the orange juice box because it said "concentrate"

Your Mum is so dumb if you gave her a penny for intelligence, you'd get change back

Your Mum is so dumb when she heard that 90% of all crimes occur around the home, she moved

Your Mum is so dumb when she took you to the airport and saw a sign that said "Airport Left" she turned around and went home

Your Mum is so dumb she ordered a cheeseburger from McDonald's and said, "Hold the cheese".

Your Mum is so dumb she returned a donut because it had a hole in it.

Your Mum is so dumb she stole free samples.

Of course, you could always focus on a mother's personal appearance

Your Mum is so ugly I told her to take out the trash and she moved out of my house

Your Mum is so ugly she looked out the window and got arrested for mooning.

Your Mum is so ugly just after she was born, her mother said "What a treasure!" and her father said "Yes, let's go bury it."

Your Mum is so ugly they filmed "Gorillas in the Mist" in her shower

Your Mum is so ugly when she walks into a bank, they turn off the surveillance cameras

Your Mum a is so ugly when she was born the doctor slapped her parents

Your Mum is so ugly she got a cease and decist letter from Sear's photography.

Your Mum is so ugly the local peeping-tom knocked on her door, and asked her to shut her blinds

Your Mum is so ugly she made an onion cry.

Your Mum is so ugly her parents had to tie a pork chop on her neck so the dog would play with her.

Your Mum is so ugly when she looks in the mirror her reflection ducks

Your Mum is so ugly, she looks like she's been bobbing for apples in hot grease

Your Mum is so ugly they feed her with a frisbee

Your Mum is so ugly she got a prescription mirror

Your Mum is so ugly she went into a haunted house and walked out with an application

Your Mum is so ugly, her passport has the disclaimer "Viewer discretion is advised"

Your Mum is so ugly that when she sits in the sand on the beach, cats try to bury her.

Your Mum is so ugly that your father takes her to work with him so that he doesn't have to kiss her goodbye.

Your Mum is's so ugly her face should be registered as a lethal weapon.

Your Mum is so ugly, she entered an ugly contest and they said sorry no professionals.

Your Mum is so ugly that your grandma dropped her at the park and got charged for littering.

Your Mum is so ugly her birth certificate was an apology from the condom factory

Your Mum is so ugly she invented blind dates.

Of course, her personal hygiene is always an option

Your Mum is so dirty she has to creep up on bathwater.

Your Mum is so dirty that she was banned from a sewage facility because of sanitation worries!

Your Mum is's so dirty, she's got more clap than an auditorium.

Your Mum is so dirty she brings crabs to the beach.

Your Mum is is like a hockey player, she only showers after three periods.

Your mum is so dirty, she uses Dr. Scholl Odour Eaters for panty liners.

Your mum is so dirty when she jumped into the ocean they volunteers were hosing down seagulls for weeks.

Shakespearian Insults

Stellar invective is not a recent phenomenon. The plays of William Shakespeare are filled with examples of fine put downs that even today, can impress. Something about insulting in a Shakespearian style add a flash of pomposity that is unrivalled.

Henry IV part I

"There is neither honesty, manhood or good fellowship in thee."

"You tread upon my patience."

"He made me mad to see him shine so brisk, and smell so sweet, and talk so like a waiting gentlewoman."

"Peace, ye fat guts."

"Why, thou clay brained guts, thou knotty pated fool, thou whoreson obscene greasy tallow catch."

"Do thou amend thy face, and I'll amend my life."

Henry IV part II:

"Your means are very slender, and your waste is great."

"You are as a candle, the better part burnt out."

"What a disgrace it is to me that I should remember your name."

"What a maidenly man at arms you have become."

"Hang yourself, you muddy conger."

"His wit's as thick as a Tewkesbury mustard."

"Thou damned tripe visaged rascal."

A Winter's Tale:

"My wife's a hobby horse."

"Thou hast need of more rags to lay on thee."

"Here comes those I have done good to against my will."

"I hate thee, pronounce thee a gross lout, a mindless slave."

"She is spread of late into a goodly bulk."

"Thou fresh piece of excellent witchcraft."

"You are rough and hairy."

"His garments are rich but he wears them not handsomely."

Othello

"You rise to play and go to bed to work."

"An index and obscure prologue to the history of lust and foul thoughts."

"Damn her, lewd minx."

Anthony and Cleopatra

"Pray you, stand farther from me."

"Die a beggar."

Coriolanus

"Boils and plagues plaster you over, that you may be abhorred farther than seen and one infect another against the wind a mile. You souls of geese that bear the shapes of men."

"I find the ass in compound with the major part of your syllables."

"More of your conversation would infect my brain."

"He's a disease that must be cut away."

"You are the must chaff, and you are smelt above the moon."

"The tartness of his face sours ripe grapes, when he walks he moves like an engine and the ground shrinks before his treading."

Macbeth

"You should be women and yet your beards forbid me to interpret that you are so."

"You egg, you fry of treachery."

"Whose horrible image doth unfix my hair and make my seated heart knock at my ribs."

"A dwarfish theif."

"All that is within him does condemn itself for being there."

Romeo and Juliet

When good manners shall lie all in one or two man's hands and they unwashed too, tis a foul thing

You kiss by the book

He is not the flower of courtesy

You ratcatcher

A plague on both your houses

Hang, beg, starve, die in the streets

Thou detestable maw, thou womb of death

The Two Gentlemen of Verona

You, minion, are too saucy

If you spend word for word with me, I shall make your wit bankrupt

She hath more hair than wit, and more faults than hairs, and more wealth than faults

She is lumpish, heavy, melancholy

Degenerate and base art thou

The Taming of the Shrew

How foul and loathsome is thine image

There's small choice in rotten apples

If I be waspish, best beware my sting

A monster, a very monster in apparel

Away, you three inch fool

Am I your bird?, I mean to shift my bush

King John

If is name be George, I'll call him Peter

So vile a lout

This bawd, this broker, this all changing word

What a fool art thou, a rampaging fool, to brag and stamp and swear

Thou odoriferous stench, sound rottenness

Thy detestable bones

Out, dunghill

There is not yet so ugly a fiend of hell as thou shall be

The Merchant of Venice

There are a sort of men whose visages do cream and mantle like a tanding pond

Gratiano speaks an infinite deal of nothing

I had rather be married to a deaths head with a bone in his mouth

A villain with a smiling cheek, a goodly apple rotten at the heart

Oh, these deliberate fools

A bankrupt, a prodigal, who dare scarce show his head on the Rialto

Soft and dull eyed fool

A stony adversary, an inhuman wretch, uncapable of pity, void and empty from any dram of mercy

Beg that thou may have leave to hang thyself

The Comedy of Errors

There's many a man hath more hair than wit

She's the kitchen wench, and all grease ; and I know not what use to put her but to make a lamp of her and run her from her own light. I warrant, her rags and the tallow in them will burn a Poland winter. If she lives till doomsday, she'll burn a week longer than the whole world.

Her complexion is like Swart, like my shoe, but her face nothing like so clean kept, for why, she sweats, a man may go over shoes in the grime of it

No longer from head to foot than from hip to hip, she is spherical, like a globe, I could find out contries in her

Dissembling harlot, thou are false in all

Julius Caesar

He is a dreamer, let us leave him

What rubbish, what offal

Where will thou find a cavern dark enough to mask thy monstrous visage

You showed your teeth like apes, and fawned like hounds and bowed like bondmen

Timon of Athens

He's opposite to humanity

That there should be small love amongst these sweet knaves, and all this courtesy, the strain of man's bred out into baboon and monkey

They were the most needless creatures living

Hoy doy, what a sweep of vanity comes this way

We may account thee a whoremaster and knave

Thou disease of a friend

His days are foul and his drink dangerous

I do wish thou were a dog, that I might love thee somthing

Were I like thee, I would throw away myself

Would thou were clean enough to spit on

I'll beat thee, but I should infect my hands

Live and love thy misery

Twelfth Night

A fellow of the strangest mind in the world

Go to, your a dry fool, I'll no more of you

He speaks nothing but madman

Observe him, for the love of mockery

You are now sailed into the north of my ladies opinion, where you will hang like an icicle on a Dutchman's beard

I can hardly forbear hurling things at him

A fiend like thee might bear my soul to hell

Fie, thou dishonest Satan

Pericles, Prince of Tyre

Courtesy would seem to cover sin

Thou art the rudeliest welcome to this world

He did not flow from honourable sources

Thou art like the harpy, which, to betray, dost with thine angels face, seize with thine eagle's talons

Your peevish chastity is not worth a breakfast in the cheapest country

The food is such as hath been belched on by infected lungs

Love's Labour Lost

The music of his own vain tongue doth ravish like enchanting harmony

A whitely wanton with a velvet brow, with two pitch balls stuck in her face for eyes

You talk greasily, your lips grow foul

A most pathetical nit

He that is likest to a hogs head

Ah, you whoreson loggerhead, you were born to do me shame

Thou halfpenny purse of wit, thou pigeon egg of discretion

He hath been five thousand years a boy

A huge translation of hypocrisy, vilely compiled, profound simplicity

Weed this wormwood from your fruitful brain

Troilus and Cressida

Why, this have not a fingers decency

Though stool for a witch

Thou sodden witted Lord

Thou has no more brain than I have in mine elbows

Thou thing of no bowels, thou

Though you bite so sharp at reasons, you are so empty of them

I had rather be a tick ina sheep than such a valiant ignorance

Thou crusty batch of nature

Why, thou full dish of fool

He has not so much brain as ear wax

Not the full package

Tuppence short of a bob.

Not the crunchiest crisp in the bag.

Not the sharpest cheese in the bin.

He is serving with old balls

A few atoms short of critical mass.

Not the brightest button in the blouse

Not the crispest shirt in the closet.

An ice bricks shy of an igloo.

A few marshmallows short of a bowl of Lucky Charms.

A few bales short of a wagon load.

A few needles short of a sewing kit.

One board member short of a quorum.

A few cracker jacks short of a full box.

A few yards short of a touchdown.

Not the sharpest pitchfork in the barn.

One slice shy of a loaf.

A few megabytes short of a gig.

A few electrons short of an isotope.

A few grapes short of a fruit salad.

A few feathers short of a duck.

Not the most absorbent sponge in the sink

An olive short of a martini.

A few carrots short of a carrot cake.

Not rowing with both oars.

A few whiskers short of a kitten.

She is Conducting without a full orchestra.

A few dollars short of a paycheck

A few Prozac short of a prescription.

A couple shakes short of a sauce bottle.

A few people short of a party.

A few leaves short of a bush.

Not the tallest tree in the forest.

Not the fastest car on the track.

A few cowboys short of a rodeo.

A few roots shy of an apple tree.

A few leftovers short of a bread pudding.

A few plums short of a pie

A few Bradys short of a bunch.

One ski short of a snowmobile.

A few fuses short of a circuit.

A tire short of an eighteen wheeler.

Doesn't have all the chairs at the table.

A few rasins short of a fruitcake.

Knitting with only one needle.

Not the brightest light in the harbor.

Not the brightest bulb in the box.

A few screws short of a hardware store.

Not the sharpest knife in the drawer.

A few cards short of a deck.

A few fries short of a Happy Meal.

A burger short of a BBQ

A few peas short of a casserole.

A few keys short of a keyboard.

Not the brightest crayon in the box.

One twist short of a slinky.

Not the sharpest tool in the shed

A few threads short of a sweater.

A few sandwiches short of a picnic.

Her Driveway doesn't quite reach the road.

Two bricks short of a load.

A few clowns short of a circus.

A few beers short of a six-pack.

Missing a few buttons on his remote control.

No grain in the silo.

Not all the soldiers are marching in line.

A few corn flakes shy of a bowl.

A few watts short of a light bulb.

Not the brightest bulb in the chandelier.

Not the quickest bunny in the forest.

A few colours short of a rainbow.

A few boats short of a fleet.

A few noodles short of a chow mein.

A few bristles short of a broom.

A few players short of a team.

Couldn't hit the floor if he fell on it.

A few sheep short of a flock.

A few gunmen short of a posse.

Not the quickest horse in the stable.

Has a full six-pack, but lacks the plastic thingy that holds them all together.

Not the fastest ship in the fleet.

Ten cents short of a dollar.

A few boxes short of a pallet.

A few grams short of a pound.

A few springs short of a mattress

A few bits short of a byte.

A spoon short of a place setting.

A horseman short of an apocalypse

You are to leadership

A lovely way to insult is to juxtaposition to opposing ideals or values in your scathing put down. Of course you can substitute leadership for any other lacking quality.

You are to leadership what Cyril Smith is to Han gliding.

You are to leadership what Dr Pepper is to medicine.

You are to leadership what vomit is to foreplay.

You are to leadership what Pol Pot was to humanitarianism.

You are to leadership what bluebeard was to marriage.

You are to leadership what the Citroen 2CV is to motor racing.

You are to leadership what Donald Trump is to race relations

You are to leadership what warts are to beauty

You are to leadership what Jamaica are to world skiing

You are to leadership what acne is to self confidence

You are to leadership what sarongs are to masculinity

You are to leadership what automated services are to conversation.

You are to leadership what San Marino is to world politics

You are to leadership what a wasp is to a picnic.

You are to leadership what playboy is to the literary canon.

You are to leadership what Jordan is to mensa.

You are to leadership what liver is to a vegan buffet

You are to leadership what Father Ted is to Catholicism

You are to leadership what Screaming Lord Sutch is to politic

You are to leadership what Loon pants are to London fashion week.

You are to leadership what Charles Hawtrey was to boxing.

You are to leadership what lard is to dieting.

You are to leadership what a bacon sandwich is to a bah mitzvah.

You are to leadership what Charles Bronson is to rehabilitation.

You are to leadership what the go compare man is to opera

You are to leadership what officer Dibble is to law enforcement

You are to leadership what captain birdseye is to the admiralty

Teacher Reports

Imagine the frustration of being a teacher. Keeping calm and positive in the face of unruly students and ever changing government policy that blames teachers rather than politicians and parents for every conceivable ill. No wonder at times their school reports can be cutting.

The improvement in his handwriting has revealed his inability to spell

He has speed on the football pitch, when running from the ball

About as energetic as an absentee miner

He would be lazy but for his absence

The tropical forests are safe when John enters the woodwork room, for his projects are small and progress is slow.

This girl is lucky to find her way home.

Johns efforts to avoid work have proved successful in every regard and he continues to flourish to this end.

For this pupil, all ages are dark

After 4 years of teaching, French remains a foreign language

Give him the job and he will finish the tools

Education has not gone to his head

He has given me a new definition of stoicism: he grins and I bear it.

Her book is immaculate, it has barely been touched.

She has exhausted all Careers Guidance Education and left us wanting.

Some students excel in the reading aspect of English, others in the writing, Sarah can do the speaking part.

Everyone has the right to misunderstand but Tom is abusing the privilege.

Your son sets low personal standards and then fails to achieve them

I suspect Jane has worked with glue rather too much

If his IQ ever reaches 40 he should sell

Printed in Great Britain
by Amazon